GIRL POWER: A JOURNAL

GiRL POWER
A JOURNAL

Encouraging Prompts and Affirmations
to Empower a Confident You

CINDY WHITEHEAD

R

ROCKRIDGE
PRESS

I'd like to dedicate this book to Briel, Lola, Mazel, Mia, Klara, Elle, Kala, Quinne, Zoe, and Minna, who continually encourage other young girls to get out there and be fearless on a skateboard.

For general information on our other products and services or to obtain technical support, please contact our Customer Care Department within the United States at (866) 744-2665, or outside the United States at (510) 253-0500.

Rockridge Press publishes its books in a variety of electronic and print formats. Some content that appears in print may not be available in electronic books, and vice versa.

TRADEMARKS: Rockridge Press and the Rockridge Press logo are trademarks or registered trademarks of Callisto Media Inc. and/or its affiliates, in the United States and other countries, and may not be used without written permission. All other trademarks are the property of their respective owners. Rockridge Press is not associated with any product or vendor mentioned in this book.

Interior and Cover Designer: Catherine San Juan
Art Producer: Hannah Dickerson
Editor: Mary Colgan
Production Editor: Ellina Litmanovich
Production Manager: Riley Hoffman

All illustrations used under license from Shutterstock.com, iStock.com and The Noun Project. Author photo courtesy of Ian Logan.

Paperback ISBN: 9781638781738

R0

CONTENTS

I AM CONFIDENT.

I AM WORTHY.

I AM STRONG.

I AM KIND.

I AM POWERFUL.

I AM LOVED.

I AM EQUAL.

I AM UNSTOPPABLE.

I AM BRAVE.

I AM

Diya Nur Aqeel

INTRODUCTION

No matter what may be happening in your life, writing things out in your journal is a great way to have fun and help remind yourself that you can be confident and assertive each day.

I am Cindy Whitehead, and I started out skateboarding at your age. At the time, I was one of the only girls at the skatepark. It could have felt very scary. Instead, I decided that wanting to skateboard outweighed my fear of being different.

WHAT IS GIRL POWER?

Girl power is a phrase that encourages and celebrates girls. When we use those words together, they remind us to be empowered, have confidence, be independent, and stay strong.

No one is born feeling confident all the time—it takes some work and a bit of practice. This journal will help teach you how to be empowered and more self-confident, and, best of all, you will learn how to own it and believe it.

HOW TO USE THIS BOOK

As you go through this book, you will come across prompts to help you feel confident and assertive, and the affirmations you see are just the start of your girl-power journey. This journal is a safe space where you can share your truth without judgment. However, this book is not a replacement for a therapist or medical support; there is no shame in seeking help from an adult you trust or a professional when life gets too stressful. Explore the pages and get excited about embracing your girl power!

PART 1

I AM ONE OF A KIND

This part of your journal is all about learning what you like and dislike, finding the things you really love to do, expressing your unique self, and so much more. Finding out that you don't need others' approval to be happy is so powerful. Understand that there is beauty in all skin tones and body sizes and shapes—these are the physical things that make you special and unique. Discovering that being different is a good thing is an amazing feeling!

DATE: 4/27/23

TODAY I FEEL: 😊 😄 😌 😢 😣 😍 😶

I AM UNIQUE BECAUSE:

I'm girly and tomboy @ the same time

Think about all the ways you are different from your family and friends. What sets you apart and makes you unique? What do you love about those things you have discovered?

I'm an Only Child and my family/friends mostly all have (a) Sibling(s)

DATE: 4/23/23

TODAY I FEEL:

I LOVE MY:

mom, DaD, food, Water

Make a list of five things you love about yourself. Don't be shy.
Think of everything from your thoughts, your actions, your body,
and more. Then write them down and be proud!

1. style

2. empathy

3. optimisim

4. Creativity

5. Kindness

DATE: ....

TODAY I FEEL:

I FEEL AWESOME ABOUT:

....

What did you do recently that made you feel awesome? Was it speaking up for yourself? Was it knowing you accomplished something you previously thought you could not?

....

....

....

....

....

....

....

....

....

DATE: ....

TODAY I FEEL: ☺ ☺ ☺ ☺ ☺ ☺ ☺

I DO NOT NEED OTHER PEOPLE'S APPROVAL FOR:

....

It is very freeing when we realize we can be our true selves and not look for approval from others. Make a list of a few things you have done without seeking approval. Circle the one that made you feel most empowered and write down why.

....

....

....

....

....

....

....

....

....

DATE: ....

TODAY I FEEL:

I EXPRESS MYSELF BY:

....

You can express yourself through words and actions, in your clothes and how you present yourself, and by sharing your feelings and emotions. Which ways do you express yourself the most?

....

....

....

....

....

....

....

....

....

DATE: ....

TODAY I FEEL: 😊 😄 😌 😣 😖 😍 😕

I AM MYSELF, AND IT FEELS:

....

You are one of a kind and being yourself means you do not change to be like everyone else. When you are your true self, what are some of the things you do to be authentic? How does it make you feel?

....

....

....

....

....

....

....

....

....

DATE: ....

TODAY I FEEL:

I KNOW I AM CREATIVE BECAUSE:

....

Creativity can help you look at things in different ways and see the various possibilities and paths in front of you. How have you used your creativity to think about situations and how you approach them?

....

....

....

....

....

....

....

....

DATE: ....

TODAY I FEEL: 😊 😄 😌 😢 😫 😍 😦

SOMETHING I AM CURIOUS ABOUT IS:

....

When you are curious, you ask questions and find new and different ways to solve problems. Your mind is active, which opens new worlds and possibilities! What kinds of things are you curious about and why? How will you feed that curiosity?

....

....

....

....

....

....

....

....

....

DATE: ....

TODAY I FEEL:

I AM ENJOYING MY JOURNEY BECAUSE:

....

What are you enjoying about your life right now? When you find yourself looking back or too far ahead, how do you ground yourself in the present?

....

....

....

....

....

....

....

....

DATE: ....

EMPOWERMENT iN THE PALM OF YOUR HAND

Place your hand palm down on this page and trace around it with a pencil or marker. Color the hand. In the palm area, write the word that you feel gives you the most power.

DATE: ....

TODAY I FEEL: 😊 😄 😁 😢 😣 🥰 😲

I AM OPEN-MINDED ABOUT:

....

Being open-minded is all about being open to new ideas, thoughts, and perspectives. What are some things you are open-minded about?

....

....

....

....

....

....

....

....

....

DATE: ....

TODAY I FEEL: 😊 😄 😋 😢 😖 🥰 😕

I BELONG ANYWHERE I GO BECAUSE:

....

You are worthy, you matter, and you belong. Have there been times when you felt like you did not belong somewhere? What can you do to remind yourself that you belong?

....

....

....

....

....

....

....

....

....

....

DATE: ....

TODAY I FEEL: 😊 😄 😋 😢 😣 😍 😳

I FIND ....**TO BE BEAUTIFUL**

What does *beautiful* mean to you? Fill this page with things you find beautiful about yourself and in your life.

....

....

....

....

....

....

....

....

....

....

DATE: ....

TODAY I FEEL: 😊 😄 😛 😢 🤢 😑 😦

I HAVE A STRONG MIND ABOUT:

....

Being strong-minded can be as simple as saying that a put-down you heard is not funny and you would like the meanness to stop. Even walking away from a bad situation is being strong-minded. Name three ways you can stay strong in a challenging situation.

1. ....
   ....
   ....

2. ....
   ....
   ....

3. ....
   ....
   ....

DATE: ....

TODAY I FEEL: 😊 😄 😁 😢 😖 🥰 😮

I AM WORTHY OF LOVE BECAUSE:

....

We are all worthy of love no matter what we look like, who we are, or where we live. Pretend your best friend is writing a description of you. From their perspective, write about your positive traits.

....

....

....

....

....

....

....

....

DATE: ....

TODAY I FEEL: 🙂 😄 😋 😢 😣 🥰 😕

I LOVE MY BODY BECAUSE:

....

We all have different bodies; no two are exactly the same. What do you love most about yours? Is it your strong legs, your eyes, or maybe your smile? Make a list of everything you love about your body.

....

....

....

....

....

....

....

....

....

DATE: ....

TODAY I FEEL:

I DID MY BEST AT:

....

Doing your best is important, even if you do not succeed at something. When did you do your best, regardless of the outcome? How did it make you feel to give it your all?

....

....

....

....

....

....

....

....

....

DATE: ....

TODAY I FEEL:

I FEEL DETERMINED TO:

....

What things have you accomplished because you were determined? What barriers did you overcome? What new things are
you determined to achieve next?

....

....

....

....

....

....

....

....

....

....

DATE: ....

TODAY I FEEL: 😊 😄 😋 😢 😣 🥰 😐

I AM GRATEFUL FOR:

....

Make a list of all the things in your life you are grateful for, both small and big!

....

....

....

....

....

....

....

....

....

....

DATE: ....

GIRL-POWER POSTER

Girl power is like a superpower. Picture what symbols, shapes, and colors a girl-power poster might use and create one here. You can color the words in bold, strong colors and add anything else you like that makes you feel brave and empowered.

GIRL POWER

DATE: ....

TODAY I FEEL: 😊 😄 😋 😢 😣 🥰 😶

I DO WHAT IS RIGHT FOR ME BECAUSE:

....

Doing what is right for you means you do not get led astray when others want to do something you feel is not right for you. What is a situation you have been in when you did what was right for you, even if it was not the popular decision?

....

....

....

....

....

....

....

....

DATE: ....

TODAY I FEEL: 😊 😄 😐 😢 😫 🥰 😶

I FEEL MY MOST AUTHENTIC WHEN:

....

Being authentic is all about being the real you. You express your feelings. You do not change your personality or opinions to make anyone else comfortable. You do not give in to peer pressure. Describe your authentic self.

....

....

....

....

....

....

....

....

....

DATE: ....

TODAY I FEEL:

I KNOW I CAN DO HARD THINGS BECAUSE:

....

Doing hard things helps you learn and grow and even makes you feel more self-confident. What hard thing are you thinking of trying? Write down what you will do to tackle it!

....

....

....

....

....

....

....

....

....

DATE: ....

TODAY I FEEL: 😊 😄 😐 😣 😖 😍 😶

I KNOW I MAKE A DIFFERENCE WHEN:

....

When you help your friends and family, stand up for yourself, or create change in your neighborhood, you are helping make a difference right where you live. What skills do you have that you can share with other people?

....

....

....

....

....

....

....

....

....

DATE: ....

TODAY I FEEL:

I AM BOLD BECAUSE:

....

Being bold means taking a stance for what you believe in. Write about a time you were bold, and what happened to make you feel and act that way. In what ways would you like to be bold moving forward?

....

....

....

....

....

....

....

....

....

DATE: ....

TODAY I FEEL: 😊 😄 😑 😢 😣 😍 😗

I DO NOT DO NEGATIVE SELF-TALK BECAUSE:

....

You are your own best friend, and best friends do not speak
unkindly about each other. Write down three things you have
thought or said about yourself that were not so nice. Then cross
them out and write down a positive phrase to replace each one.

1. ....

   ....

   ....

2. ....

   ....

   ....

3. ....

   ....

   ....

DATE: ....

TODAY I FEEL: 😊 😄 😋 😢 😣 😍 😮

I BELIEVE IN "THE POWER OF YET" BECAUSE:

....

Knowing that we cannot do something right now but believing we can learn to achieve it in the future is the power of yet. Make a list of things you can't do right now, then write the word *yet* after each one.

....

....

....

....

....

....

....

....

DATE: ....

TODAY I FEEL: 🙂 😄 😝 😢 😟 🥰 😦

I FEEL MOST POSITIVE WHEN:

....

Positivity is a great way to turn negative feelings into good ones.
List the times in your life when being positive made a difficult
situation better.

....

....

....

....

....

....

....

....

....

....

DATE: ....

ONE STEP AT A TIME

The journey you are on to girl power takes many small steps to get there. Once you get to the top, it will be so worth it! Finish drawing the staircase, then color the steps in different colors and write a girl-power goal for yourself in each one. Then add yourself reaching the top!

FEEL UNSTOPPABLE

A mantra is something you can say over and over to empower yourself. It's a phrase you can use daily to give yourself a boost of confidence! You can do this in your bedroom or in your family's bathroom. Look straight into the mirror and see everything that is strong and beautiful about you. Feel your power. Let that feeling course through your body all the way down to your toes. Now say out loud, "I am powerful, I am strong, I am unstoppable, I am brave, and I have serious GIRL POWER!"

MEGAN RAPINOE

Megan Rapinoe (1985–) is an American professional soccer player. She is known for her activism and for being an outspoken LGBTQ advocate. Megan uses her soccer legacy and fame to stand up for groups that are continually marginalized by society.

AMANDA GORMAN

Amanda Gorman (1998–) is the youngest inaugural poet in US history. She read her poem "The Hill We Climb" at the 2021 inauguration, when Joe Biden became the 46th president of the United States. Amanda is known as a "change maker" because she uses the power of her words to make people listen and help create change.

PART 2

I AM (GIRL) POWERFUL

Let's learn about building your confidence, embracing challenges, and finding out how to be in touch with your thoughts and feelings. You will find out that you have the resilience to face anything that comes your way. You will also learn that building a community with other girls enhances your girl power! Here is where you really get to shine, explore, and feel powerful.

DATE: ....

TODAY I FEEL: 😊 😃 😐 😢 😫 😍 😶

I CAN DO ANYTHING BECAUSE:

....

If you believe in yourself, you really can do anything you set your mind to. What are some of the things you want to try or do? Make a list here so you can look at it anytime you want to remind yourself to smash some goals.

....

....

....

....

....

....

....

....

....

DATE: ....

TODAY I FEEL: 😊 😀 😬 😢 😖 😍 😕

I WAS STRONG WHEN:

....

Heading out into the world and having strength in what you believe gives you a great foundation to feel confident. When you speak up and do what it takes to help, you are showing the world your strength. Think of some things that make you feel strong and write them down.

....

....

....

....

....

....

....

....

....

DATE: ....

TODAY I FEEL: 🙂 😄 😁 😢 😖 😍 😮

I AM RESILIENT BECAUSE:

....

Resilience helps you bounce back from things that do not go your way. It can be anything from staying positive after losing a game, to brushing off an awkward comment. How do you practice resilience in your life?

....

....

....

....

....

....

....

....

....

DATE: ....

TODAY I FEEL:

I AM CONFIDENT WHEN:

....

Being confident shows people that you believe in yourself and you believe in what you say and do. What are some things you are confident about?

....

....

....

....

....

....

....

....

....

....

DATE: ....

TODAY I FEEL: 😊 😄 😠 😣 😫 😍 😶

I AM IN CONTROL BECAUSE:

....

When you are in a stressful situation and you feel in control, you can stay calm and make better decisions. Learning to be in control takes some practice. Quiet your mind, breathe, and think calmly about what is happening. List three ways you can help yourself stay in control.

1. ....

....

....

2. ....

....

....

3. ....

....

....

DATE: ....

TODAY I FEEL: 🙂 😄 😋 😣 😖 😍 😶

I AM KIND BECAUSE:

....

When we show kindness to others, we lift them up, and as a result, we rise, too. There is serious girl power in numbers! How have you shown kindness to others this week? What was the outcome?

....

....

....

....

....

....

....

....

DATE: ....

TODAY I FEEL:

I FELT I CREATED CHANGE WHEN:

....

Creating change is a powerful feeling. Name something you'd like to create change about and write it below. Then write out the ways you can make that happen.

....

....

....

....

....

....

....

....

....

....

DATE: ....

TODAY I FEEL: 😊 😁 😐 😣 😫 😍 😵

I AM SURE OF MY ABILITIES BECAUSE:

....

Being sure of your abilities is another kind of girl power. You know you can do something. Why? Because you have confidence in yourself, and you will figure it out and make it happen. What abilities are you confident about? How did you put them to use this week, and how did it make you feel?

....

....

....

....

....

....

....

....

....

DATE: ....

TODAY I FEEL:

I CAN SAY NO BECAUSE:

....

Do you sometimes have a hard time saying no? Make a list below of some things you can practice saying no to—you can start small, like saying no to hanging out today. You can work up to a bigger scenario, such as saying no if someone asks you to do something you are not comfortable with.

....

....

....

....

....

....

....

....

....

DATE: ....

YOU ARE A SUPERHERO

Draw yourself as a superhero! Design your own outfit and don't forget to give yourself a rad superhero cape. Then fill the rest of the page with words and symbols that remind you of your girl-power strength.

DATE: ....

TODAY I FEEL: 🙂 😄 😋 😢 😣 🥰 😐

I AM POWERFUL WHEN:

. . . .

You have so much power. Think about all the ways you can use it.
You can help change what is wrong in the world, make someone
smile, or bring people together. How do you use your power? Are
there new ways you want to use your power going forward?

. . . .

. . . .

. . . .

. . . .

. . . .

. . . .

. . . .

. . . .

. . . .

DATE: ....

TODAY I FEEL:

I FEEL PEACEFUL WHEN:

....

Sit and close your eyes for a few minutes. Relax and let the calm flow through you. Now open your eyes and write down five other ways you can help yourself feel calm and peaceful during the day.

1. ....

2. ....

3. ....

4. ....

5. ....

DATE: ....

TODAY I FEEL:

I FORGIVE OTHERS BECAUSE:

....

Forgiveness is a powerful thing. When we can forgive others, it helps us feel closure and a sense of peace. Name some things that have happened that upset or hurt you, but that you were able to forgive and move on from.

....

....

....

....

....

....

....

....

DATE: ....

TODAY I FEEL:

I AM GENEROUS ABOUT:

....

You can be generous with your time, share something you have, teach someone a new skill, and so much more. Write about a time when you were generous. How did it make you feel?

....

....

....

....

....

....

....

....

....

DATE: ....

TODAY I FEEL: 🙂 😀 😋 😢 😖 😍 😑

I AM SMART BECAUSE:

....

Being smart is not just about things you learn in school each day. It also has to do with making good decisions for yourself even if others do something different. Write down the ways you were smart this week.

....

....

....

....

....

....

....

....

....

DATE: ....

TODAY I FEEL: 🙂 😀 😋 😢 😣 😍 😐

I AM EMPOWERED WHEN:

....

You can feel empowered when you do things like let people know how you want to be treated, speak up about things that matter to you, and much more. When have you felt empowered?

....

....

....

....

....

....

....

....

....

DATE: ....

TODAY I FEEL: 🙂 😄 😝 😣 😫 🥰 😑

I STAND UP FOR MYSELF BECAUSE:

....

Standing up for yourself takes courage. Think about the times
when you stood up for yourself. Why did you need to do it? Was
it hard? Did you feel good after you did it? What happened next?

....

....

....

....

....

....

....

....

....

DATE: ....

TODAY I FEEL: 😊 😀 😛 😔 😣 🥰 😶

I CHOOSE MY WORDS WISELY BECAUSE:

....

Your words have power. You can make someone feel good or feel hurt, depending on what words you use. How do you want to make people feel with your words? Write down five sentences you could use to have a positive impact when speaking to someone.

1. ....

....

2. ....

....

3. ....

....

4. ....

....

5. ....

....

DATE: . . . .

TODAY I FEEL:

I AM CONFIDENT WHEN:

. . . .

Looking people in the eye, speaking clearly, voicing your opinion, and standing tall—these are all behaviors that show others you have confidence. What are some other actions you can name that let people know you are a confident individual?

. . . .

. . . .

. . . .

. . . .

. . . .

. . . .

. . . .

. . . .

DATE: ....

YOU ARE POWERFUL

The Sun is powerful, just like you. Write your name in the circle, then draw rays to make the circle into a colorful sun. Next, write all the things that make you unique and strong in the Sun's rays. Read it out loud when you are done and see how strong and powerful you are!

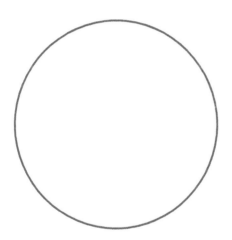

DATE: ....

TODAY I FEEL:

I AM ALWAYS LEARNING BECAUSE:

....

Every day you learn something new. Try and think about all the new things you have learned this week and write them down. You will be surprised at just how much you learned.

....

....

....

....

....

....

....

....

....

DATE: ....

TODAY I FEEL: 😌 😁 😐 😣 😢 😍 😑

TODAY I OVERCAME MY FEAR BY:

....

It is natural to feel fear. Facing your fear can be empowering. Write down three things that make you feel uncomfortable. Then, one at a time, cross them out and write down a way in which you can turn that fear into power.

1. ....

....

....

2. ....

....

....

3. ....

....

....

DATE: ....

TODAY I FEEL: 😊 😄 😌 😢 😖 🥰 😎

I BELIEVE IN MYSELF BECAUSE:

....

Believing in yourself means being confident in your abilities. Can you think of a time when you believed in yourself? What happened? How did it make you feel?

....

....

....

....

....

....

....

....

....

....

DATE: ....

TODAY I FEEL: 😊 😁 😛 😢 😟 😍 😮

TODAY I MADE A DIFFERENCE BY:

....

Making a difference can be through the big or small things you do. What are some ways you can make a difference for your family, your friends, your class, and your community?

....

....

....

....

....

....

....

....

....

....

DATE: ....

TODAY I FEEL: 🙂 😄 😐 😢 😫 😍 😶

I HAVE PURPOSE BECAUSE:

....

When you have a strong drive in your life that keeps your focus, that is having purpose. It could be scoring that soccer goal or landing that kickflip on your skateboard. How do you live your life with purpose? What does it feel like?

....

....

....

....

....

....

....

....

....

DATE: ....

TODAY I FEEL: 😊 😄 😋 😢 😖 😍 😎

I CAN ACCEPT COMPLIMENTS BECAUSE:

....

Accepting compliments comes from being secure in who you are. You have the power to accept those kind words and know you deserve the praise. Name some compliments you have been given. How do they make you feel?

....

....

....

....

....

....

....

....

....

DATE: ....

TODAY I FEEL: 🙂 😄 😋 😢 😟 🥰 😶

TODAY I MADE TIME FOR MYSELF BY:

....

Making time for you is important. Do you notice how you feel calmer and your thoughts are clearer when you take a bubble bath or do yoga in your room? Make a list of the things you like to do for yourself and how they make you feel.

....

....

....

....

....

....

....

....

....

DATE: ....

TODAY I FEEL:

TODAY I WAS PRESENT DURING:

....

Being present means that you are paying attention to what is happening in the moment rather than thinking about the past or the future. At what times are you fully in the moment? How can you be present more often?

....

....

....

....

....

....

....

....

....

DATE: ....

GiRL-POWER PATCH

Design a Girl-Power patch! Use any colors, words, or symbols that make you feel strong.

BREATHE IN CALMNESS AND BREATHE OUT STRESS

Sit on the floor or on your bed with your legs crossed. Get comfy. Now close your eyes and take slow breaths, in and out. Feel yourself becoming calm and relaxed. Think about any issues or unresolved problems you may have had this week. With each breath, exhale the problem away. This is a great way to end your day or week with positivity!

SUSAN B. ANTHONY

Susan B. Anthony (1820–1906) was a women's rights activist and social reformer. She played a huge role in the women's suffrage movement. Her work helped pave the way to give American women the right to vote in 1920.

SIMONE BILES

Simone Biles (1997–) is considered one of the greatest gymnasts of all time. Simone pulled out of her events during the 2020 Olympics due to the "twisties," a mental block when a gymnast loses track of space and timing when spinning through the air. Her brave decision to prioritize her mental health over medals opened up a larger conversation about mental health issues.

PART 3

I AM BRAVE & COURAGEOUS

Bravery is like a muscle you need to work. The more you work it, the stronger it gets. When you start taking actions that enforce courage rather than fear, you will learn that all kinds of cool things happen. You will stretch yourself to be honest with yourself and others. You start becoming a leader, but you also encourage others to do the same. Being brave helps you be more independent and less reliant on others.

DATE: ....

TODAY I FEEL:

I AM BRAVE BECAUSE:

....

Being brave is about standing up for what you believe in, standing up for others (and yourself), and having the courage to be honest and vulnerable. Whew! What else does bravery mean to you? Describe your bravest moment.

....

....

....

....

....

....

....

....

DATE: ....

TODAY I FEEL: (͡° ͜ʖ ͡°) (͡° ͜ʖ ͡°) (͡° ͜ʖ ͡°) (͡° ͜ʖ ͡°) (͡° ͜ʖ ͡°) (͡° ͜ʖ ͡°) (͡° ͜ʖ ͡°)

I CAN OVERCOME FEAR BECAUSE:

....

Everyone is afraid of something, but you can also channel that fear and make it into your power by facing it bit by bit. Write down one thing you fear and think of three steps you can take to start to overcome it. If you can tackle each piece by itself, it doesn't seem as scary overall.

....

....

....

....

....

....

....

....

....

DATE: ....

TODAY I FEEL:

I AM COURAGEOUS BECAUSE:

....

Think about some things you have done even though you were afraid. Being courageous means you push past your fears and go after what you want. Write a list of goals that make you fearful, but that you'd like to have the courage to accomplish anyway.

....

....

....

....

....

....

....

....

....

DATE: ....

TODAY I FEEL: 😊 😬 😌 😢 😣 😍 😦

I AM TRUSTWORTHY BECAUSE:

....

Being on time, not talking about people behind their backs, following through on commitments—these are actions that demonstrate your trustworthiness. Write down the ways you show others that you are trustworthy.

....

....

....

....

....

....

....

....

....

DATE: ....

TODAY I FEEL:

I AM HONEST WITH MYSELF AND OTHERS BECAUSE:

....

It takes bravery to be honest with yourself and others. Write about a time you had the courage to be honest. Was it difficult? How did it make you feel?

....

....

....

....

....

....

....

....

....

DATE: ....

TODAY I FEEL: 😊 😄 😬 😢 😣 🥰 😐

I TRUST MYSELF BECAUSE:

....

When was the last time you trusted yourself to make a difficult decision? What was it about? How did it make you feel knowing that you trusted your decision? Write it all down.

....

....

....

....

....

....

....

....

....

....

DATE: ....

TODAY I FEEL:

I CAN BE PERSISTENT ABOUT:

....

When you are persistent, you do not give up easily. Sometimes our persistence pays off, and sometimes we have to keep trying. Think of one goal you have and identify an obstacle that is standing in your way. Write down how you can be persistent in overcoming it.

....

....

....

....

....

....

....

....

....

DATE: ....

TODAY I FEEL: 😊 😄 😌 😢 😍 🥺

I FEEL READY TO:

....

Feeling ready is when you are mentally prepared to do what you want to accomplish. How do know when you are ready for something? How does it feel in your body and your mind?

....

....

....

....

....

....

....

....

....

....

DATE: ....

TODAY I FEEL: 😊 😄 😣 😢 😖 😳 😘

WHEN I STAND UP FOR OTHERS, I FEEL:

....

Standing up for others shows that you care and that they do not need to stand alone. When we help each other out like this, we all become stronger. Write about a time when you stood up for someone else. How did it make you feel before, during, and after?

....

....

....

....

....

....

....

....

....

DATE: ....

I CAN SAY NO

Draw yourself as your own cheerleader, in any type of outfit you like. Picture yourself: You are strong, courageous, and able to use the word *no* when you need to.

DATE: ....

TODAY I FEEL:

I KNOW I CAN CHANGE MY FEELINGS BECAUSE:

....

Write down situations where you may have reacted too fast in anger, and then write down ways you could have changed that mindset.

....

....

....

....

....

....

....

....

....

DATE: ....

TODAY I FEEL: 🙂 😄 😊 😢 😣 🥰 😮

I DREAM BIG BECAUSE:

....

When we dream, we imagine all the things that we can do in life. It takes courage to dream big. What are some of your big dreams?

....

....

....

....

....

....

....

....

....

DATE: ....

TODAY I FEEL: 🙂 😄 😑 😢 😖 😍 😕

I FORGIVE MYSELF BECAUSE:

....

Having the courage to forgive yourself is an important part of your growth. It is much braver to forgive yourself and move forward than to dwell on what you may have done wrong. Write about a time when you had the courage to forgive yourself.

....

....

....

....

....

....

....

....

DATE: ....

TODAY I FEEL:

I SHOW COMPASSION TOWARD OTHERS WHEN:

....

When you show compassion, you make others feel better about whatever they may be going through. What are some of the ways you show compassion for others?

....

....

....

....

....

....

....

....

....

....

DATE: ....

TODAY I FEEL: 🙂 😄 😁 😢 🤢 😍 😳

I LEARN FROM MY MISTAKES WHEN:

....

Everyone makes mistakes, and that is okay! Write down some of your most memorable mistakes and, next to them, write down what you learned from each one.

....

....

....

....

....

....

....

....

....

....

DATE: ....

TODAY I FEEL: 😊 😄 😁 😢 😖 😍 😨

I KNOW THAT I CAN OVERCOME DIFFICULTIES BECAUSE:

....

Everyone has difficulties in their life. Sometimes they are small, like fixing a broken bike. Other times they are larger. Think of one difficulty, either small or large, that you were able to overcome. What did you learn that will help you overcome other difficulties in the future?

....

....

....

....

....

....

....

....

....

DATE: ....

TODAY I FEEL: 😊 😄 😌 😢 🤢 🥰 😐

I RESPECT MYSELF BECAUSE:

....

When you respect yourself, you do things that are good for you and help you grow. What are some ways that you show respect for yourself?

....

....

....

....

....

....

....

....

....

DATE: ....

TODAY I FEEL: 😊 😄 😌 😢 😖 🥰 😵

I CHOOSE TO SPEAK WITH KINDNESS BECAUSE:

....

When you speak with kindness, you show the world that you are a strong and secure person. Write about a time someone spoke to you with kindness or a time you showed kindness to someone else.

....

....

....

....

....

....

....

....

DATE: ....

TODAY I FEEL: 🙂 😄 😢 😣 😖 😍 😦

I AM POSITIVE ABOUT:

....

When we choose positive thoughts and emotions over negative ones, we feel better and react to the world in more productive ways. Write about some negative thoughts, then reframe them as positive thoughts to help you practice positive thinking.

....

....

....

....

....

....

....

....

....

DREAM BIG(GER)

Fill this field with trees stretching up to the sky and then add lots of clouds. Draw clouds that are big enough to fit your dreams. Inside those puffy clouds, write down dreams you have for yourself.

DATE: ....

TODAY I FEEL: 🙂 😄 😕 😢 😣 😍 😐

I FEEL SAFE BECAUSE:

....

To feel safe, we need to have firm boundaries, speak up when
needed, make mistakes freely, and know that we are loved no
matter what. Write about a place where you feel safe. What
makes it a safe place for you?

....

....

....

....

....

....

....

....

....

DATE: ....

TODAY I FEEL:

I AM A LEADER BECAUSE:

....

Think of someone in your life, like a friend, teacher, or parent, who you think is a good leader. What are some qualities that you admire about them? Which of these qualities do you share? Which ones would you like to develop?

....

....

....

....

....

....

....

....

....

....

DATE: ....

TODAY I FEEL:

I AM MINDFUL ABOUT MY FEARS BECAUSE:

....

When we tap into our courage as a mindful response to our fears, we can respond to what scares us instead of running away from it. This is where bravery comes in. Think about times when you were afraid and write down ways you were mindful about that fear and what the outcome was when you faced it logically.

....

....

....

....

....

....

....

....

....

DATE: ....

TODAY I FEEL: 🙂 😁 😌 😢 😣 😍 😮

I KNOW I CAN BE VULNERABLE BECAUSE:

....

Vulnerability is you opening yourself up completely and allowing others in. It can be a bit scary, but it is part of growing to become stronger. Can you think of times when you have allowed yourself to be vulnerable? How did it feel to let people in?

....

....

....

....

....

....

....

....

....

DATE: ....

TODAY I FEEL: 🙂 😄 😐 😢 😠 😍 😵

I AM THE ARCHITECT OF MY LIFE BECAUSE:

....

This is your life, and you get to build it from the foundation up. Each day, you add pieces that help you grow and shape your life however you want. Write your personal story about how you are shaping your life in the direction you want it to go.

....

....

....

....

....

....

....

....

....

DATE: ....

TODAY I FEEL: 🙂 😄 😊 😢 😠 😍 😮

I SHARE MYSELF FEARLESSLY BECAUSE:

....

When you express yourself without worrying about what other people think—this is sharing yourself fearlessly. Write about times when you have shared yourself fearlessly and how it felt.

....

....

....

....

....

....

....

....

....

DATE: ....

TODAY I FEEL: 😊 😁 😝 😢 😖 🥰 😳

I WILL FIGURE IT OUT BECAUSE:

....

Sometimes we don't know things, and that is okay. Figuring it out means you will do what it takes to understand, solve, or find the answer. Write about something you didn't know how to do and how you were able to figure it out.

....

....

....

....

....

....

....

....

....

DATE: ....

TODAY I FEEL: 🙂 😁 😋 😢 😣 😍 😳

I SHOW PEOPLE WHO I AM WHEN:

....

The way you talk, how you behave, and how you treat yourself and others are all ways you show others who you are. What are some other ways you show people who you are? How does it make you feel?

....

....

....

....

....

....

....

....

....

YOU CAN FIGURE IT OUT

Use these lines as a starting point to draw something that reminds you of being brave.

PUNCH IT OUT

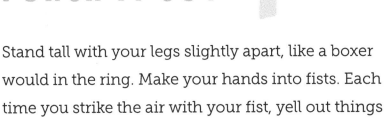

Stand tall with your legs slightly apart, like a boxer would in the ring. Make your hands into fists. Each time you strike the air with your fist, yell out things that make you feel brave. Do five punches and then take a rest. Do as many rounds as you wish!

RUTH BADER GINSBURG

Ruth Bader Ginsburg (1933–2020) was the first Jewish woman appointed to the US Supreme Court. She was a champion of gay rights, women's rights, the poor, and many other marginalized groups. Ruth said, "Fight for the things that you care about, but do it in a way that will lead others to join you."

GLORIA STEINEM

Gloria Steinem (1934–) is an American feminist journalist and social-political activist. Her career path started when she was just a teen. Gloria felt that her mother was not treated well by her male employers simply because she was a woman. Gloria created change and became known in the 1960s as a leader of the feminist movement.

PART 4

I AM ENOUGH

It is time to celebrate you and keep loving the strong, worthy person you are! You know you are enough, and you feel comfortable saying it. You have learned how to express your feelings, and you love yourself just the way you are, physically, mentally, and emotionally. Being able to accept yourself completely gives you more time and energy to give and receive and uplift other girls. That is a great feeling!

DATE: ....

TODAY I FEEL: 😊 😄 😌 😢 😫 🥰 😵

I AM ALLOWED TO BE MYSELF BECAUSE:

....

When we give ourselves permission to be who we really are physically, mentally, and emotionally, it is a freeing feeling. How are you feeling about being your true self right now?

....

....

....

....

....

....

....

....

....

DATE: ....

TODAY I FEEL: 🙂 😀 😌 😢 😣 😍 😮

I AM SELF-AWARE BECAUSE:

....

To be self-aware means to see yourself clearly and to understand your own thoughts and feelings. Writing in a journal is a great way to gain self-awareness. Use this page to "free write," or write about anything that comes to mind. Did anything surprise you?

....

....

....

....

....

....

....

....

....

DATE: ....

TODAY I FEEL:

I AM BALANCED BECAUSE:

....

Feeling balanced means feeling calm and safe. Your thoughts are in order. You feel rested and can make good decisions. Think of a time when you felt rested. Write about what it was like for you physically and emotionally. How often do you feel rested?

....

....

....

....

....

....

....

....

....

DATE: ....

TODAY I FEEL:

I AM CALM BECAUSE:

....

Make a list of the ways you help yourself stay calm when things are tough. Circle the ways that work best for you.

....

....

....

....

....

....

....

....

....

....

DATE: . . . .

TODAY I FEEL:

I AM ENOUGH BECAUSE:

. . . .

You are enough! You know that being yourself is plenty, and you do not need to be anyone but you. What are some things about you that you like and that make you know deep inside that you are enough?

. . . .

. . . .

. . . .

. . . .

. . . .

. . . .

. . . .

. . . .

DATE: ....

TODAY I FEEL:

I AM FEELING FREE BECAUSE:

. . . .

When was the last time you felt like nothing was weighing you down? You were not worried. You felt comfortable in your own body and free to express your true thoughts and feelings. Write a paragraph about that experience and how you got there.

. . . .

. . . .

. . . .

. . . .

. . . .

. . . .

. . . .

. . . .

. . . .

DATE: ....

TODAY I FEEL: 🙂 😀 😁 😭 😣 😍 😶

I KNOW I AM GROWING BECAUSE:

....

You are growing right now. You have used this journal to learn more about yourself, your feelings, and how to help other girls rise with you. Can you share below all the ways you feel that you have grown while writing in your journal?

....

....

....

....

....

....

....

....

....

DATE: ....

TODAY I FEEL: 🙂 😄 😐 😢 😣 😍 😕

I LOVE MYSELF BECAUSE:

....

It is important to be loving toward other people, but it is also important to love yourself. What are some ways that you show love to yourself? How can you do this more?

....

....

....

....

....

....

....

....

....

....

DATE: ....

TODAY I FEEL: 🙂 😄 😊 😣 🤢 😍 😶

I DESERVE HAPPINESS BECAUSE:

....

What makes you happy? Make a list long enough to fill this page.
Look back at it often and remember that you deserve happiness!

....

....

....

....

....

....

....

....

....

REACH FOR THE SKY

Start with the tree trunk, and then draw in the rest of the
tree with lots of strong branches reaching high into the sky.
As you draw each branch, think about your strengths and
all the things you have learned recently that helped you
grow. Then write strong words about yourself on the leaves.

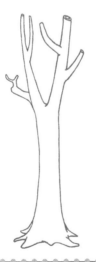

DATE: ....

TODAY I FEEL: 😊 😄 😋 😢 😫 🥰 😳

I AM BEAUTIFUL INSIDE AND OUT BECAUSE:

....

Knowing that you are beautiful is about acknowledging that every single part of you that is unique makes you beautiful. Take a minute to write down all the qualities you have—inside and out—that make you beautiful.

....

....

....

....

....

....

....

....

....

DATE: ....

TODAY I FEEL: 😊 😀 😄 😢 😫 😍 😮

I AM EMPOWERED BY:

....

Feeling empowered is you taking ownership of your life. You
know that what you feel is right for you, and you feel comfortable expressing that. Write a paragraph about when you felt your
most empowered this week.

....

....

....

....

....

....

....

....

....

DATE: ....

TODAY I FEEL: 😊 😄 😌 😢 🤢 😍 😳

I KNOW I AM LOVED BECAUSE:

....

Everyone deserves to be loved for being who they are. Name some people who have made you feel loved. Write down every name you can think of. Anytime you get down on yourself, look at this list and know you are loved!

....

....

....

....

....

....

....

....

....

DATE: ....

TODAY I FEEL:

I AM HAPPY BECAUSE:

....

Make a list of things, big and small, that made you happy today.

....

....

....

....

....

....

....

....

....

....

DATE: ....

TODAY I FEEL: 🙂 😀 😐 😢 😫 😍 😳

I AM PERFECTLY IMPERFECT, AND THAT IS OKAY BECAUSE:

....

No one is perfect. We all make mistakes, and that is part of grow-ing. Being perfectly imperfect is wonderful, so embrace it! What makes you perfectly imperfect? How does being perfectly imper-fect make you feel?

....

....

....

....

....

....

....

....

....

DATE: ....

TODAY I FEEL:

I PRACTICE SELF-COMPASSION BECAUSE:

....

Forgiving yourself is a great way to show self-compassion. Write below about times when you were hard on yourself unnecessarily. Now that you know self-compassion is important, what would you tell yourself today?

....

....

....

....

....

....

....

....

....

DATE: ....

TODAY I FEEL: 🙂 😀 😐 😢 🤢 😍 😶

I AM WHOLE BECAUSE:

....

Being whole is all about you embracing who you are. You embrace the good things as well as the things that you are working on or toward. Share a specific time when you felt like you knew you were whole.

....

....

....

....

....

....

....

....

....

DATE: ....

TODAY I FEEL: 🙂 😄 😊 😢 😣 🥰 😶

I MAKE TIME TO CARE FOR MYSELF BECAUSE:

....

Caring for yourself is important, not only for your body but also your mind. When you make time to care for yourself, you treat yourself with compassion and respect. What are some things you do to practice self-care?

....

....

....

....

....

....

....

....

....

DATE: ....

TODAY I FEEL:

I LOVE THE SKIN I AM IN BECAUSE:

....

Loving exactly who you are is so important to your girl power. You do not see flaws; you see the beauty in your unique self. You stand tall and embrace who you are—every part of you. Name all the things you love about yourself and why.

....

....

....

....

....

....

....

....

....

DATE: ....

LET'S BE PERFECTLY iMPERFECT

Use this page to draw a picture of yourself. Don't go back and erase or change anything as you draw. There are no mistakes here. Just keep drawing. Now look at your finished work. This work is unique, just like you. Do you see how there is beauty in being perfectly imperfect?

DATE: ....

TODAY I FEEL: 😊 😄 😐 😢 😩 🥰 😳

I CAN LET GO OF WHAT NO LONGER WORKS FOR ME BECAUSE:

....

What are some things you can let go of? How would it feel to release yourself from these things? If you give yourself permission to remove the things that weigh you down, it allows you to focus on the good stuff.

....

....

....

....

....

....

....

....

DATE: ....

TODAY I FEEL:

I CHOOSE TO CELEBRATE MY LIFE BECAUSE:

....

It is time to celebrate you! At times, you will smash bigger goals and celebrate, but what about the small things you accomplish each day? Those are worth celebrating as well. How do you celebrate your life?

....

....

....

....

....

....

....

....

DATE: ....

TODAY I FEEL: 😊 😄 😋 😢 😖 🥰 😳

I LISTEN TO MY HEART BECAUSE:

....

Listening to your heart means trusting your feelings and instincts.
Can you think of a time when you made a decision by listening
to your heart? How do you feel about what happened after your
decision?

....

....

....

....

....

....

....

....

....

DATE: ....

TODAY I FEEL: 🙂 😄 😐 😢 🤢 😍 😕

I RADIATE CONFIDENCE BECAUSE:

....

Radiating confidence shows those around you that you are self-assured and know who you are. There are also times you will need to tap into your girl power and tell yourself, "You got this!" Write about a time when you just knew that you radiated confidence.

....

....

....

....

....

....

....

....

....

DATE: ....

TODAY I FEEL: 🙂 😄 😆 😣 😖 😍 😋

I DO NOT JUDGE MYSELF BECAUSE:

....

Judging yourself is like having a frenemy who points out your
mistakes. No one wants that. Write down things you judged
yourself about in the past, and then write down some loving
comments that change judgment to self-love.

....

....

....

....

....

....

....

....

DATE: ....

TODAY I FEEL: (emoticon faces)

I PUT MYSELF AND MY NEEDS FIRST BECAUSE:

....

Putting yourself first is not selfish. It is an important step in taking care of your body and mind and having time alone with your thoughts and feelings. How do you put yourself and your needs first?

....

....

....

....

....

....

....

....

....

DATE: ....

TODAY I FEEL: 🙂 😄 😌 😣 😫 🥰 😶

I LOVE MYSELF MORE EACH DAY BECAUSE:

....

Finding things to love about yourself shows that you are learning
about who you want to be. What are some ways you can con-
tinue to grow and change? Keep adding to this page day after
day to see them all add up.

....

....

....

....

....

....

....

....

....

DATE: ....

TODAY I FEEL: 😊 😄 😌 😢 😣 😍 😦

MY NAME IS ....,

AND I AM ENOUGH, JUST THE WAY I AM,

RIGHT IN THIS VERY MOMENT (AND FOREVER)!

....

....

....

....

....

....

....

....

....

....

DATE: ....

BECAUSE I'M HAPPY!

In the 10 boxes below, draw one thing in each box that makes you happy—from big to small, leave nothing out. Use this page as a reminder that you have so many things in your life to celebrate and be happy about.

CELEBRATION DANCE

You can do this in your room or outside if the weather is nice. Put on your favorite music and start dancing. As you move your body to the music, think of all the things you celebrate about yourself and how far you have come. Keep dancing until the end of the song, and if you need more time to celebrate, play it on repeat!

SERENA WILLIAMS

Serena Williams (1981–) is an American professional tennis player, fashion designer, and philanthropist. She is widely regarded as one of the greatest female tennis players of all time. Serena has often spoken out about women's rights and equality.

MAYA ANGELOU

Maya Angelou (1928–2014) was an American poet, memoirist, and civil rights activist. She received dozens of awards and more than 50 honorary degrees. Maya was respected as a spokesperson for Black people and women.

RESOURCES

Girls Can't WHAT? challenges girls to break through gender stereotypes and achieve their dreams. GirlsCantWhat.com/blog

Girls Inc. helps girls learn to value themselves, take risks, and discover and develop their inherent strengths. GirlsInc.org

Girls Leadership teaches girls to exercise the power of their voice through programs grounded in social and emotional learning. GirlsLeadership.org

Strong Is the New Pretty by Kate T. Parker celebrates, through more than 175 memorable photographs, the strength and spirit of girls being 100 percent themselves.

ABOUT THE AUTHOR

 **Cindy Whitehead** is a professional skateboarder, writer, and activist. At 15, she had a two-page article and centerfold in a skateboarding magazine, where she spoke out about being one of the only girls in a male-dominated sport. She is the author of two books and runs the movement Girl is NOT a 4 Letter Word. Her skateboarding history sits in the Smithsonian National Museum of American History's Sports Collections. Cindy was inducted into the Skateboarding Hall of Fame in 2016.

CPSIA information can be obtained
at www.ICGtesting.com
Printed in the USA
JSHW080725291222
35316JS00003B/4